For You

FOR CHANTELLE A.
THIS IS FOR YOU.

NEW BEGINNINGS
Published by LHC Publishing 2021

Text Copyright © 2021 Y. Eevi Jones
Illustrations Copyright © 2021 Y. Eevi Jones
Cover Design by Y. Eevi Jones
Cover Art by Olga Matyash

Printed in the USA.

All inquiries should be directed to
www.LHCpublishing.com

ISBN-13: 978-1-952517-11-2 Paperback
ISBN-13: 978-1-952517-10-5 Hardcover

Life's Biggest Moments

NEW BEGINNINGS

My New Chapter in Life

WRITTEN BY
EEVI JONES

My Sweet Self:

Some things are meant to last.
Some things are meant to end.
Some things can be rebuilt and fixed,
while others we cannot mend.

Our true self, hidden for years
below veils of habit and grind,
has begun to reach for the light
to be heard and be less confined.

An unexpected yesterday
may have caused a hard today.
May linger through tomorrow.
May leave. Or it may stay.

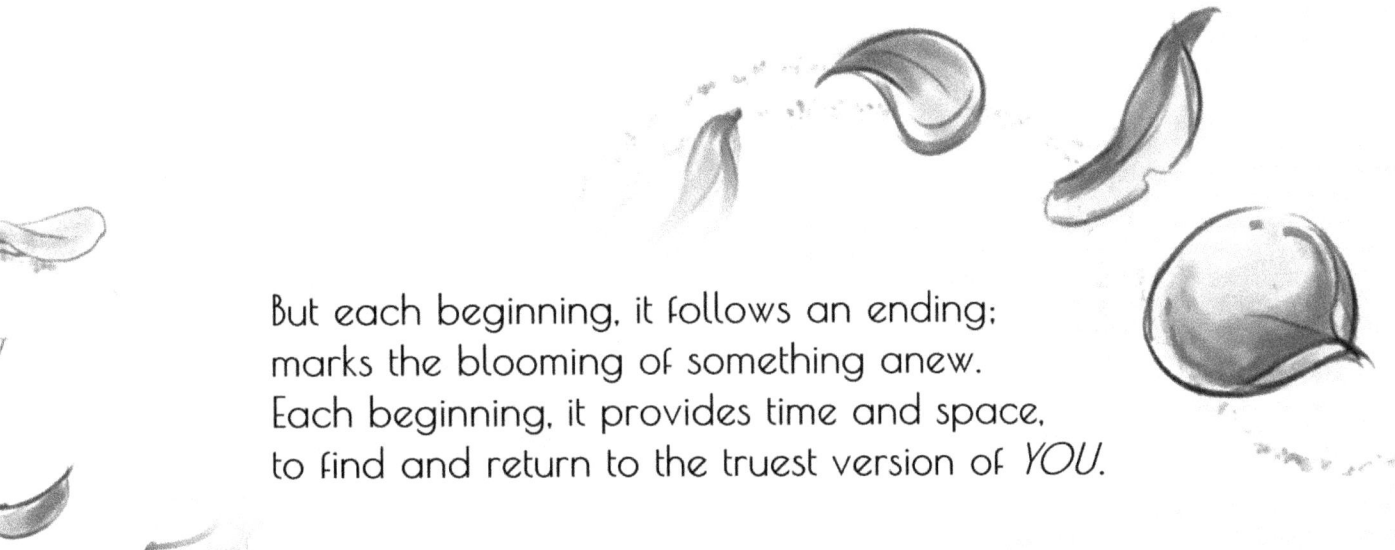

But each beginning, it follows an ending;
marks the blooming of something anew.
Each beginning, it provides time and space,
to find and return to the truest version of *YOU.*

Today it may be hard.
Today it may be tough.
Today you may think and feel
that you are not enough.

With broken promises and hearts,
broken trust and bond,
the healing seems so distant.
Unthinkable. Beyond.

Yet, the hurt, the blame, the aching,
albeit felt this very hour,
is temporary only,
and soon will lose its power.

Hang on! Hang tight my dear!
Push through the veil of tears.
Push through regret and rue.
Push through the sheets of fears.

The fears of being lonely,
the fears of the unknown,
are fears meant for the past alone.
And the past you have outgrown.

For today is the day where we begin to invite
all the wanted, the better, the more.
Today is the day where we will forgo
all the guilt and hurt we so felt before.

Less times already past.
More moments yet to come.
Less gray. Less dull. Less gloom.
More rays of warmth and sun.

More what you want. Less what you should.
More rainbows over rain.
More what brings joy. Less what brings none.
More of the new, not the mundane.

More speaking through your soul,
less through your words alone.
More compassion toward another's heart.
More compassion toward your own.

More hands that want to hold.
Hold tight, and don't let go.
More arms providing warmth.
Warmth felt from head to toe.

More respect, appreciation.
For one another. A give and take.
More passion, smiles, laughs.
More good for goodness' sake.

More paths that lead together.
More talks that share the *YOU*.
More nights of walks and gazing
into skies of midnight blue.

More honesty, more candor.
More of the here and now.
Less dwelling on the past.
Less of the why and how.

You get to tune and you get to set
the strings, the rules, the time.
You get to toss and you get to keep,
to start living by design.

Times of yore and yesterday
are tucked away now nice and tight.
Making room for new tomorrows
that are worthy, true, and bright.

So today, go choose yourself.
Choose changes over none.
For your new and marvelous life
has only just begun.

ABOUT THE AUTHOR

Writing under a number of pen names, Eevi Jones is a USA Today & WSJ bestselling and award-winning author and ghostwriter of children's books.

Born in former East Germany to a German mother and a Vietnamese father, Eevi loves to infuse her children's books with racial diversity. Always drawing inspiration from her own two children, she writes about unique interests and aspires to find fun and exciting ways to have kids discover and learn about the magnificent marvels this world has to offer.

Eevi has been featured in Forbes, Scary Mommy, Business Insider, Huffington Post, Exceptional Parent Magazine, and more.

She can be found online at www.BravingTheWorldBooks.com.

A WORD BY THE AUTHOR

New beginnings are often intertwined with hurt, doubt, and many shed tears. Yet, I hope that with this book, you come to see that new beginnings also bring hope, joy, and self-love, providing us with an opportunity to find, rediscover, and love our own true selves. Life has so much in store for us. We just have to allow it in.

If you enjoyed this book, it would mean the world to me if you would take a short minute to leave a heartfelt review. Thank you.

OTHER WORKS BY THIS AUTHOR

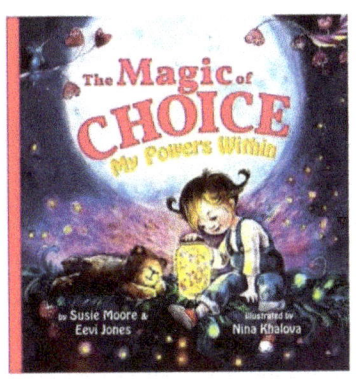

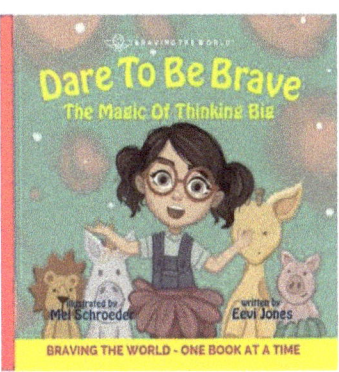

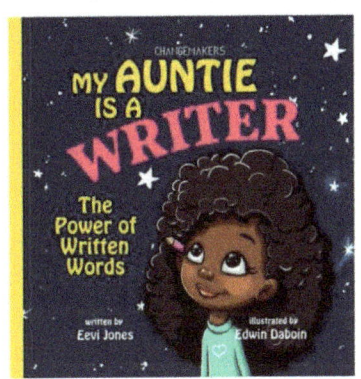

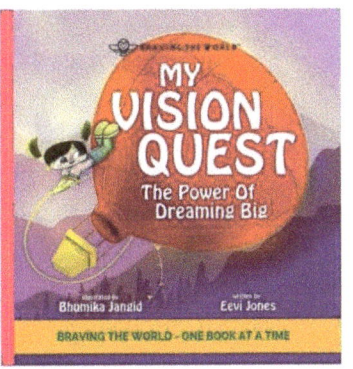

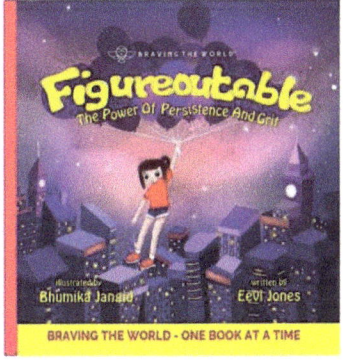

... AND MANY MORE

NEW BEGINNINGS - RESOURCES

Whatever you are currently feeling, please know that you're NOT alone.

Below, I've provided a link to a number of wonderful resources and Facebook communities that are specifically for those who need support during this time of their lives. Ending a chapter in our lives and beginning a new one can be a very lonely experience, and having someone to share our thoughts and feelings with can help us go through this process.

http://www.bravingtheworldbooks.com/new-beginnings-resources

www.ingramcontent.com/pod-product-compliance
Lightning Source LLC
LaVergne TN
LVHW070121100526
838202LV00011B/327